Current Events: Decoding the Conflict Between Israel and the Palestinians

About Charles River Editors

Charles River Editors was founded by Harvard and MIT alumni to provide superior editing, writing, and admissions consulting services with the domain experience your project needs. Our team includes management consultants, post-doctoral researchers, practicing engineers, practicing lawyers, practicing physicians of numerous specialties, and finance professionals. In addition to providing digital content for other publishers, we also self-publish original academic content and public domain classics.

Visit charlesrivereditors.com for more information.

Introduction

In May 2011, President Barack Obama gave speeches about the Middle East that discussed the Israeli-Palestinian conflict, using terms like "final status issues," "1967 lines with mutually agreed swaps," and "demographic realities." Obama's speeches were strongly denounced by both the Palestinians and the Israelis, while political commentators across the world debated what Obama's speeches actually meant.

Welcome to the Middle East conflict, a conflict that is technically 63 years old and counting but has its roots in over 2,000 years of history. With so much time and history, the peace process has become laden with unique, politically sensitive concepts like the right of return, contiguous borders, secure borders, demilitarized zones, and security requirements, with players like the Quartet, Palestinian Authority, Fatah, Hamas, the Arab League and Israel. Over time, it has become exceedingly difficult for even sophisticated political pundits and followers to keep track of it all.

Until now. ***Decoding the Conflict Between Israel and the Palestinians*** cannot solve the peace process, nor does it heap credit or blame on any of the sides. This book goes about breaking down all the terms often thrown around in the Middle East that make the peace process a political minefield, and one that both beginners and sophisticated followers have a hard time keeping up with. Serving as both a glossary and primer of the history of the Middle East conflict and the peace process, ***Decoding the Conflict between Israel and the Palestinians*** defines the terms, looks at the region's history, discusses previous attempts at negotiations like Oslo and Taba, identifies important figures, and explains the arguments and mentalities of each side, showing why the conflict has proven so intractable.

Along with analysis, anecdotes, and dozens of maps and pictures of important events and people, *Decoding the Conflict between Israel and the Palestinians* will get you up to speed on the history of the Middle East conflict and serve as a reference point that will help keep you updated as events in the region unfold.

Chapter 1: Palestine under Ottoman Rule

Nearly a century before the state of Israel was founded in 1948, Palestine was under the control of the Ottoman Turkish Empire, consisting mostly of Arabs. During the 1850s, Jews began settling in small villages across the lands that once comprised Judea and Samaria, which the Jews considered their ancient Biblical homeland.

These efforts to buy property were driven by the motivation of some Jews to help reestablish the land as the Jewish homeland. These Jews became known as **Zionists**, in reference to Zion, which is often thought of as a reference to all of Israel but was in fact a reference to part of Jerusalem. The Zionists attempted to establish a Jewish National Fund that would assist Jews in buying land in Palestine for Jewish settlement.

Zionism as a political movement gathered steam in the 1890s, supported by Zionists, led by **Theodore Herzl,** who wished to found a Jewish state for the Jews in Palestine. The creation of a Jewish homeland also enjoyed strong support from many Christians who saw the reestablishment of Israel as fulfilling Biblical prophecy.

Leading up to World War I, Zionists across Europe and the United States began lobbying their countries for support to help reestablish a Jewish homeland.

Key Terms:

Diaspora – The term that refers to the expulsion and movement of Jews out of Ancient Israel, beginning with its conquest by the Roman Empire, who occupied Israel and renamed it Palestine after the Philistines, who had historically been the Jews' adversaries.

Theodore Herzl

Chapter 2: World War I and the Balfour Declaration

During World War I, the Ottoman Turks joined the Central Powers against the Allies, which consisted of Great Britain, France, Russia, and later the United States. The fighting spanned the entire European continent, but it also raged across Turkey and the Middle East. British official T. E. Lawrence, better known as Lawrence of Arabia, went to Mecca, where he worked on causing dissension within the Ottoman Empire.

In the middle of World War I, the British pledged their support to the Zionist cause and the establishment of a Jewish state in Palestine through the **Balfour Declaration** of November 1917. At the time, the British realized the strategic importance of Palestine because it was near the Suez Canal, and they saw the Zionists as potentially helpful allies in the region following the war. British foreign secretary Arthur James Balfour sent a letter to Lord Rothschild on November 2, 1917, declaring the government's "sympathy with Jewish Zionist aspirations," and favoring "the establishment in Palestine of a National Home for the Jewish People," with an intent to assist the Jews in achieving it.

It is a common misconception that the Europeans and the United States created Israel in response to the Holocaust, sympathizing with the plight of the Jews. There's no question that empathy with the Jews occurred because of historic anti-Semitism in Europe during the 19th and early 20th centuries, but the Balfour Declaration essentially guaranteed the modern State of Israel 27 years before the end of World War II.

Foreign Office,
November 2nd, 1917.

Dear Lord Rothschild,

I have much pleasure in conveying to you, on behalf of His Majesty's Government, the following declaration of sympathy with Jewish Zionist aspirations which has been submitted to, and approved by, the Cabinet

"His Majesty's Government view with favour the establishment in Palestine of a national home for the Jewish people, and will use their best endeavours to facilitate the achievement of this object, it being clearly understood that nothing shall be done which may prejudice the civil and religious rights of existing non-Jewish communities in Palestine, or the rights and political status enjoyed by Jews in any other country"

I should be grateful if you would bring this declaration to the knowledge of the Zionist Federation.

The Balfour Declaration

Chapter 3: The British Mandate for Palestine

The Ottoman Empire quickly collapsed after World War I, and its extensive lands were divvied up between the French and British. While the French gained control of the Levant, which would later become modern day nations like Syria, the British were given the **Mandate for Palestine** from the newly created League of Nations.

The British Mandate for Palestine gave the British control over the lands that have since become Jordan, Israel, the West Bank, and the Gaza Strip. The terms of the British Mandate incorporated the language of the Balfour Declaration, recognizing the "historical connection of the Jewish people with Palestine." The British were also tasked with creating a Jewish state, which the United States Congress endorsed in 1922.

During 1920, riots broke out in the Mandate that inflamed tensions between the Jews and Arabs. In response, in 1921 the British carved a large section out of the Mandate to establish the state of Transjordan, better known today simply as **Jordan**. Jordan comprised over 75% of the lands of the British Mandate. The following year, the **Churchill White Paper** banned Jews from immigrating into Jordan, thereby ensuring that its population would be heavily Hashemite and Palestinian.

Throughout the 1930s, there were restrictions on Jewish immigration to the British Mandate, which inadvertently consigned millions of European Jews to death in the Holocaust. Nevertheless, from 1918 to 1945 thousands of Jews made their way to the British Mandate.

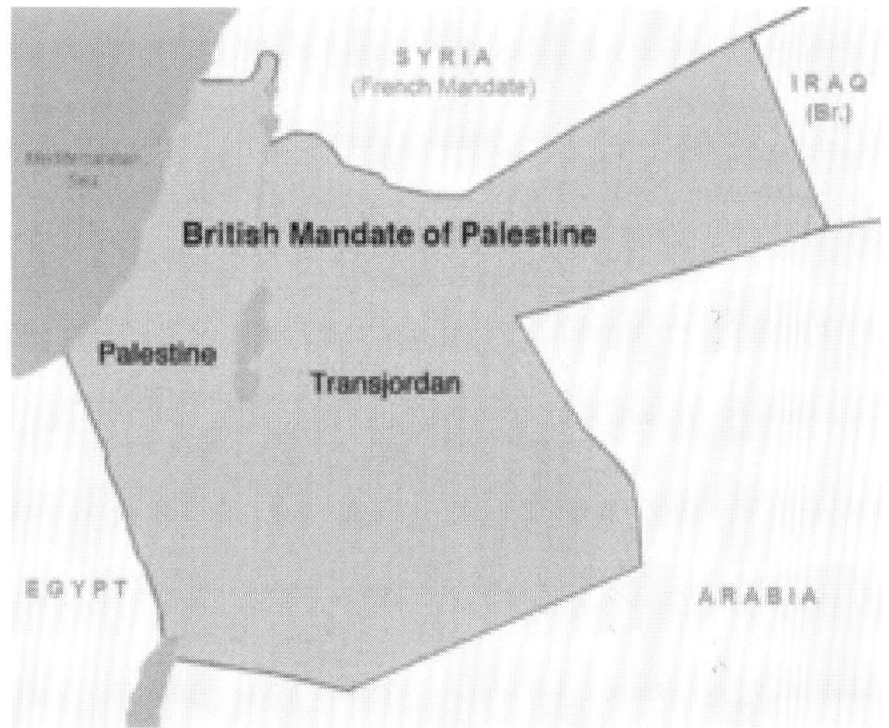

The British Mandate of Palestine. After the creation of Transjordan, Zionists were upset at what they felt was a betrayal of the principles of the Balfour Declaration. At the same time, as discussed next chapter, the United Nations Partition Plan would give more than half of the remaining 23% of the British Mandate to Israel, which would upset the Palestinians.

Even today, many Israeli politicians and supporters argue that a Palestinian state already exists in Jordan, and that the creation of Palestine would essentially create a second Palestinian state. For decades, Israeli politicians sought to have the Palestinian conflict resolved by having Jordan assimilate the Palestinians, under a plan known as the Allon Plan.

Chapter 4: The United Nations Partition Plan

Tensions between Jews and Arabs persisted throughout the Middle East, and the Zionists were growing exceedingly frustrated with the British, who had created Transjordan and were limiting Jewish immigration. As a result, Zionist militias, including the **Haganah** and **Irgun**, began attacking British targets in the 1940s. The most famous act of terrorism took place on July 22, 1946, when the Irgun blew up a section of the King David Hotel, killing nearly 100 people. Jewish terrorism in Palestine compelled the British to disentangle themselves from the British Mandate, but the Jews and Arabs were not able to formalize any deal for carving up the remaining portion of the Mandate into two separate states.

In 1947, the British delegated the issue of partitioning the British Mandate to the United Nations, and the U.N. General Assembly set up the Special Committee on Palestine (UNSCOP). UNSCOP eventually came up with what is now known as the **U.N. Partition Plan of 1947:**

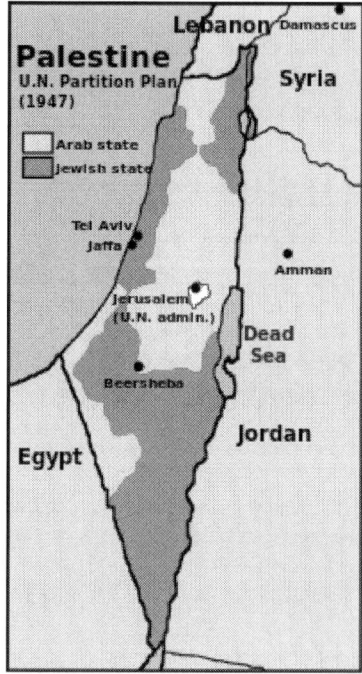

The Partition Plan carved up two strange looking states, but their motive was to create an Israel in which the Jewish population was a 55% majority, while Palestine had an over 90% Palestinian

Arab majority. Meanwhile, the city of Jerusalem would be administered internationally, due to the sensitive religious concerns of Muslims, Christians, and Jews. In addition to several Christian holy spots, Jerusalem's Al-Aqsa Mosque is the third holiest site in Islam, and it is situated right next to the Western Wall, the Jews' holiest remaining site.

The proposed plan was accepted by the Jewish Agency, which represented the leaders of the Jewish community in Palestine. However, it was rejected by Palestinian leaders in the Mandate, and it was also rejected by the newly formed Arab League, a confederation of Middle Eastern Arab states led by Egypt, Lebanon, Iraq, Saudi Arabia, Syria, and Yemen. Although the partitioned state of Israel would have had a Jewish majority, the remainder of the British Mandate after the partition of Jordan was about 2/3 Palestinian, and they viewed the plan as being unfairly advantageous to the Jews.

The British were still in control of the Mandate, and they accepted the U.N. Partition Plan, but they had no interest in attempting to enforce the partition of the two states, especially not over the objections of one side after British forces had already been subjected to violence by Jewish groups. And without the British, there was no way for the United Nations to enforce the partition.

Therefore, in September 1947, the British announced that they would be wiping their hands clean of the entire Mandate on May 14, 1948.

Important Terms:

After the Six Day War in June 1967, Israel came into control of the Gaza Strip and the West Bank, lands that were to comprise part of the state of Palestine under the U.N. Partition Plan. They are most frequently referred to as the **Palestinian Territories** or **Occupied Territories** by the Palestinians and the international community. Some people still refer to them as the **Disputed Territories**, since the U.N. Partition Plan that called for them to be Palestinian territories was never formally accepted by the Palestinians themselves.

Chapter 5: The 1948 War

On May 14, 1948, the British Mandate officially expired. That same day, the Jewish National Council issued the *Declaration of the Establishment of the State of Israel*. About 10 minutes later, President Truman officially recognized the State of Israel, and the Soviet Union also quickly recognized Israel.

However, the Palestinians and the Arab League did not recognize the new state, and the very next day, armies from Egypt, Syria, Lebanon and Iraq invaded the former British Mandate to squelch Israel, while Saudi Arabia assisted the Arab armies. Jordan would also get involved in the war, fighting the Israelis around Jerusalem. Initially, the Arab armies numbered over 20,000 soldiers, but the Zionist militia groups like the Lehi, Irgun and Haganah made it possible for Israel to quickly assemble the Israel Defense Forces, still known today simply as the **IDF**. By the end of 1948, the Israelis had over 60,000 soldiers and the Arab armies numbered over 50,000.

The Israelis began pressing their advantages on both land and air by the fall of 1948, bombing foreign capitals like Damascus while overrunning Arab armies in the British Mandate. In towns like Ramat Rachel and **Deir Yassin**, close quarter combat in villages led to civilian casualties and charges of massacres. In particular, the Jewish assault on Deir Yassin, which led to the death of about 50 Palestinians, is often labeled a massacre by the Palestinians, although the Israelis asserted that house to house combat made fighting difficult.

Regardless, Palestinians who heard of the news of Jewish attacks on places like Deir Yassin were afraid for their lives and began to flee their homes. At the same time, Palestinians were encouraged by commanders of the Arab armies to clear out of the area until after they could defeat Israel. Palestinians and Jews had been fighting since 1947, and over 250,000 Palestinians had already fled their homes by the time the 1948 War had started. It is unclear how many Palestinians fled from Jewish forces and how many left voluntarily, but by the end of the war over 700,000 Palestinians had fled from their homes in the former British Mandate. Meanwhile, nearly 800,000 Jews had been forcibly expelled from their homes in nations throughout the Middle East, leading to an influx of Jews at the same time Palestinians were leaving.

In late 1948, Israel was on the offensive. That December, the U.N. General Assembly passed **Resolution 194**, which declared that under a peace agreement, "refugees wishing to return to their homes and live in peace with their neighbors should be permitted to do so," and "compensation should be paid for the property of those choosing not to return." Months later, Israel began signing armistices with Egypt, Jordan, and Syria, which left Israel in control of nearly 75% of the lands that were to be partitioned into the two states under the 1947 plan. Jordan now occupied Judea and Samaria, which later became known as the West Bank due to its position on the western bank of the Jordan River. Jordan also occupied three quarters of

Jerusalem, with the Israelis controlling only about a quarter in the western part of the city. To the west, Egypt occupied the Gaza Strip.

The new armistice lines became known as the **"Green Line."**

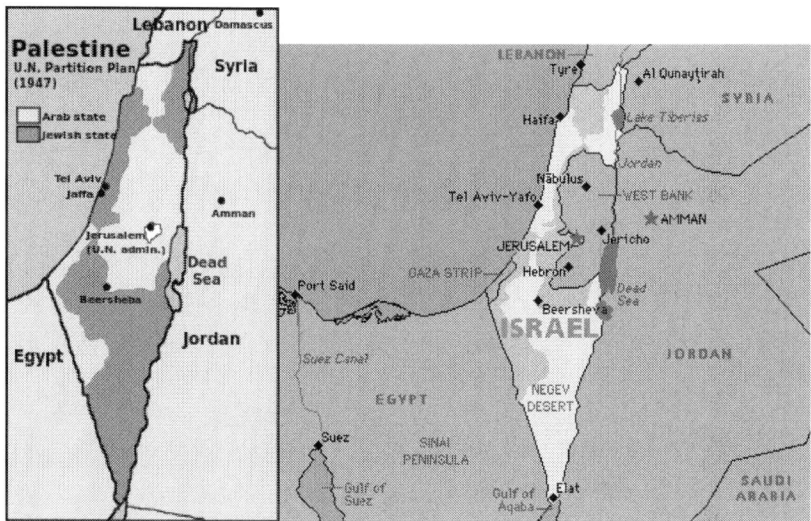

On the right, the large gains made by Israel after the end of the 1948 War are apparent.

The Palestinians and their supporters often argue that Palestinian refugees have the right to return to their land under General Assembly Resolution 194. The Israelis and their supporters assert that Resolution 194 requires a peace agreement and that the refugees who are to return must wish to live in peace.

The issue of the Palestinian refugees is now one of the biggest points of difference between Israel and the Palestinians. The Palestinians claim the right of all the descendants of the original 700,000 Palestinian refugees to return to their original homes. That number is now almost 5 million, which would give the Palestinians a majority in Israel and demographically end the Jewish state. Israel rejects an unlimited right of return, of course, but, as discussed further in detail throughout this book, it is politically infeasible for Palestinian leaders to negotiate any limitation on the right of return.

Each May 14, the Palestinians commemorate the "Nakba," or catastrophe. The "Nakba" is commemorated to mourn what befell the Palestinian refugees, but the Israelis and their supporters point out that the Palestinians commemorate the Nakba on the day Israel declared its independence, thus making them believe the Palestinians consider Israel's independence the catastrophe.

Sometimes, pro-Palestinian commentators or Palestinian politicians will assert that the Palestinians' quest for a state in the West Bank and Gaza Strip only represent 22% of the total Palestinian homeland, and thus the Palestinians have already made generous concessions to Israel. The West Bank and Gaza Strip represent more than 50% of the proposed state of Palestine under the 1947 Partition Plan, whereas the territories represent 22% of the entire British Mandate after Jordan had been carved out of it. In essence, they are stating that the creation of the State of Israel itself was a concession.

Chapter 6: The Palestine Liberation Organization

In 1964, the Arab League met in Cairo and formed the **Palestine Liberation Organization** (PLO), which intended to "liberate" Palestine and drive the Jews into the sea. At the time, Egypt and Jordan occupied the Gaza Strip and West Bank respectively, which the PLO had no interest in contesting. The PLO Charter stated, "This Organization does not exercise any territorial sovereignty over the West Bank in the Hashemite Kingdom of Jordan, or on the Gaza Strip."

Although the PLO became the most famous Palestinian organization, it actually consisted of several independently operating groups. The most noteworthy of them was **Fatah**, which had been founded in 1956 and had been conducting attacks on Israeli targets since its inception. Among the members of Fatah was **Yasser Arafat**, who would soon become the most visible face of the PLO. Other main groups within the PLO included Popular Front for the Liberation of Palestine and the Popular Democratic Front for the Liberation of Palestine, which essentially were militant groups.

Yasser Arafat became chairman of the PLO in 1968, making him the de facto leader of the Palestinians. Yasser Arafat's PLO was not just unpopular among Israelis: his group fought against the Jordanians and groups in Lebanon throughout the 1970s and 1980s, before being allowed back into the Gaza Strip and West Bank during the Oslo Peace Process of the 1990s.

Chapter 7: The Six Day War

Israel and its neighbors continued sporadic fighting with each other, including the Suez Canal War in 1956. But it was in 1967 that the map would drastically change once again.

Despite losing the 1948 war, Arab nations throughout the Middle East had still refused to recognize Israel's right to exist. After the Suez Canal War, Egyptian leader **Gamal Abdel Nasser** envisioned creating a unified Arab world, commonly referred to as pan-Arabism. Nasser was the consummate pan-Arab leader in the 1960s, positioning himself as the leader of the Arab world through increasing incitement against Israel with rhetoric.

Israel found itself in possession of more land after 1948 than envisioned by the U.N. Partition Plan, but the Green Line still left it less than 10 miles wide in some positions. In the summer of 1967, the armies of Jordan and Syria mobilized near Israel's borders, while Egypt's army mobilized in the Sinai Peninsula just west of the Gaza Strip. Combined, the Arab armies numbered over 200,000 soldiers.

In early June 1967, the Israelis captured Jordanian intelligence that indicated an invasion was imminent. On June 5, the Israelis launched a preemptive attack that knocked out the air forces of its Arab neighbors. Over the next six days, the Israelis overwhelmed the Egyptians in the west, destroying thousands of tanks and capturing the Gaza Strip and the entire Sinai Peninsula. At the same time, Israel drove the Jordanians out of Jerusalem and the West Bank, and it captured the Golan Heights from Syria near the border of Lebanon.

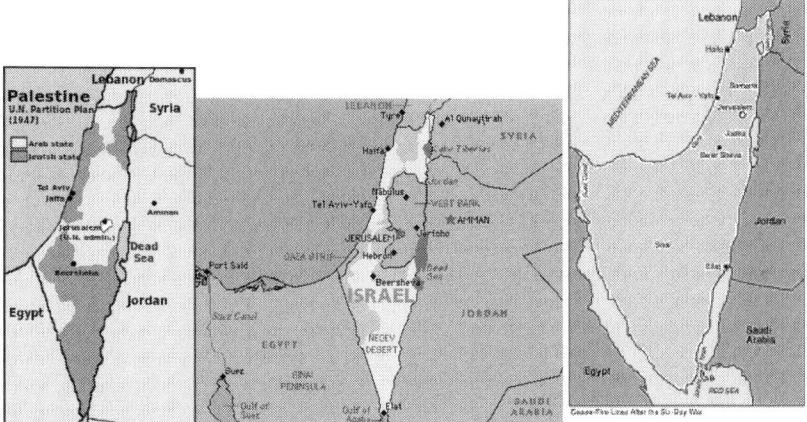

In the span of a week, Israel had tripled the size of the lands it controlled. Israel had gone from less than 10 miles wide in some spots to over 200 miles wide from the Sinai Peninsula to the West Bank. Israel also unified Jerusalem.

As with the 1948 war, the 1967 war ended with an armistice, creating war heroes out of **Yitzhak Rabin** and **Ariel Sharon**.

Chapter 8: U.N. Security Council Resolution 242

The results of the Six Day War created several issues that have still not been resolved in the Middle East. Israel now found itself in possession of territories that were the home of over a million Arabs. Of these territories, Israel officially annexed only East Jerusalem and the Golan Heights, leaving the inhabitants of the West Bank, Sinai Peninsula, and Gaza Strip in limbo regarding citizenship status.

On November 22, 1967, the United Nations Security Council passed **Resolution 242**, still one of the central resolutions of the conflict. Creating the "land for peace" formula, the resolution called for "[t]ermination of all claims or states of belligerency and respect for and acknowledgment of the sovereignty, territorial integrity and political independence of every State in the area and their right to live in peace within secure and recognized boundaries free from threats or acts of force."

In exchange for the Arab nations ending their belligerency and acknowledging Israel's sovereignty, Resolution 242 called for the "[w]ithdrawal of Israel armed forces from territories occupied in the recent conflict." This is one of the most important and most misunderstood aspects of the resolution. Although a simple reading of the language seems to call upon Israel to return to the Green Line and give back all of the lands captured during the Six Day War, the U.N. diplomats did not intend for that. The language intentionally left out the word "the" in front of the word territories, an indication that the resolution did not call upon Israel to return to the Green Line before the Six Day War of 1967.

Resolution 242 was drafted by the British, whose U.N. Ambassador, Lord Caradon, later said, "It would have been wrong to demand that Israel return to its positions of June 4, 1967, because those positions were undesirable and artificial. After all, they were just the places where the soldiers of each side happened to be on the day the fighting stopped in 1948. They were just armistice lines. That's why we didn't demand that the Israelis return to them."

Similarly, the American U.N. Ambassador said, "The notable omissions – which were not accidental – in regard to withdrawal are the words "the" or "all" and the "June 5, 1967 lines" ... the resolution speaks of withdrawal from occupied territories without defining the extent of withdrawal... Israel's prior frontiers had proved to be notably Insecure."

Despite misconceptions and misinterpretations of Resolution 242, it became essential to the subsequent formulation of the peace processes that launched in the 1990s and used the pre-1967 borders as the starting point for negotiating final borders.

Chapter 9: Israel's Settlements

Despite attempts to create peace, the Arab nations refused to recognize Israel, and Israel refused to withdraw from any of the land it captured in 1967. After conquering the territories, Israel began encouraging Jewish settlement in the new territories. In the 1970s, more than 10,000 Jews moved into the West Bank, Gaza Strip, Golan Heights, East Jerusalem, and the Sinai Peninsula, a figure that grew to over 100,000 by the early '80s and is now over 500,000 today.

Some in Israel note that Jewish settlements in 1967 had simply reestablished Jewish communities in places they had lived prior to 1948, including Jerusalem, Hebron, and Gush Etzion, as well as Gaza City in the Gaza Strip. They also argue that the legal status of the territories was never officially determined due to the Palestinian rejection of the U.N. Partition Plan. Still others assert that Israel's settlements do not breach international law or the Geneva Convention because it fought the Six Day War in self-defense and did not forcibly transfer civilian populations onto occupied territories.

However, despite those arguments, the vast majority of the world considers Jewish settlements on land captured by Israel in 1967 to be illegal, including the United Nations, the International Court of Justice, and the international community.

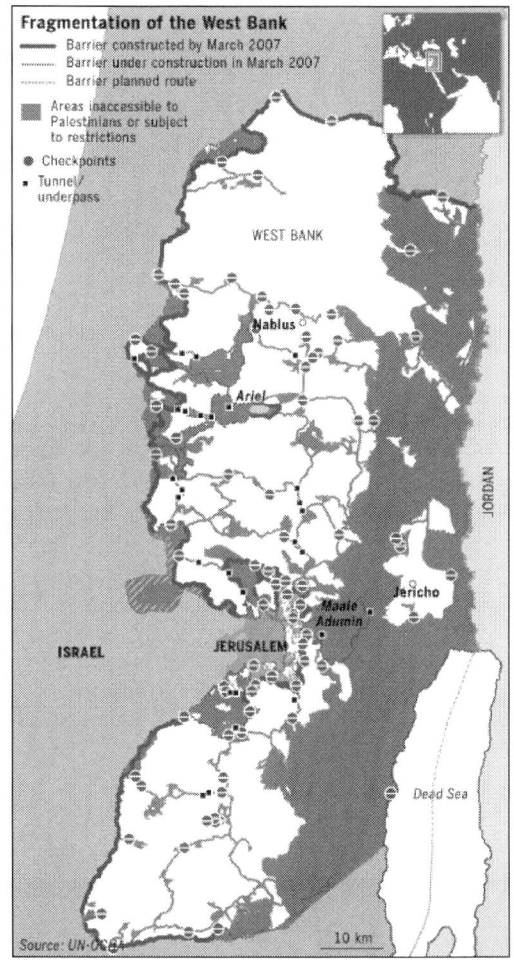

As will be discussed further in depth later, aside from Ariel, Israel's main settlement blocs in the West Bank mostly hew to the Green Line and the borders of Jerusalem. Israel also controls the Valley of the Jordan River, which they claim is necessary to prevent the militarization of the area through weapons smuggling or the entry of a foreign nation's forces.

Chapter 10: The Camp David Accords of 1978

On October 6, 1973, Syria and Egypt caught Israel off guard during the Jewish holy holiday of Yom Kippur, surprise attacking the Sinai Peninsula and Golan Heights. Although they initially made gains, the Israelis turned the tide within a week, going on the counteroffensive and winning the war within 3 weeks.

The Yom Kippur War was the last concerted invasion of Israel by conventional Arab armies, but it underscored how entangled the West and the Soviet Union had gotten in the region. The British and French had been allied with Israel in the 1950s, including during the Suez Canal War, and the United States assisted Israel by providing weapons as early as the 1960s. As a way of counteracting Western influence, the Soviets developed ties with the Arab nations.

After the Yom Kippur War, President Carter's administration sought to establish a peace process that would settle the conflict in the Middle East, while also reducing Soviet influence in the region. On September 17, 1978, after secret negotiations at the presidential retreat Camp David, Egyptian President Anwar Sadat and Israeli Prime Minister Menachem Begin signed a peace treaty between the two nations, in which Israel ceded the Sinai Peninsula to Egypt in exchange for a normalization of relations, making Egypt the first Arab adversary to officially recognize Israel. Carter also tried to create a peace process that would settle the rest of the conflict vis-à-vis the Israelis and Palestinians, but it never got off the ground.

For the Camp David Accords, Begin and Sadat won the Nobel Peace Prize. Begin had once been a leader of the paramilitary group Irgun, while Sadat had succeeded Nasser. The peace treaty cost Sadat his life: he was assassinated in 1981 by fundamentalist military officers during a victory parade.

The military officers had ties to the opposition group **Muslim Brotherhood**, as well as Ayman al-Zawahiri, who later became one of the leaders of al-Qaeda.

Begin, Carter and Sadat at the signing ceremony

Chapter 11: Fighting in Lebanon

While Israel was negotiating a peace with Egypt, it continued to combat the PLO, which was staging attacks from Palestinian refugee camps in Lebanon. In 1978, Israel occupied the southern part of Lebanon in order to create a buffer security zone. But in 1982, Israel invaded Lebanon, and at the same time Syrian forces were fighting Lebanese forces during Lebanon's Civil War. The result was a witch's brew of interconnected alliances between forces in Lebanon, which consisted of Shiite militias, Sunni militias, Christian militias, Druze militias, the newly formed **Hezbollah**, Syria, Lebanon and Israel.

Israel and Syria had still not reached peace, making them adversaries in Lebanon. Israel was allied with the Phalangist Christian militia, which not only attacked Syrians but also Palestinians after the assassination of Bachir Gemayel, the former Phalangist leader who was president elect of Lebanon in September 1982.

The Lebanon Civil War is mostly known in the United States and France for the attacks on its barracks that killed hundreds of members of the U.N.'s international peacekeeping force. In the Middle East, the most notorious attack was the **Sabra and Shatila massacre**, carried out by the Phalangists against Palestinian refugees in the two refugee camps to avenge the assassination of Gemayel. As the Phalangists killed hundreds, the IDF surrounded the perimeter. The IDF did not directly participate, but an Israeli investigation held Defense Minister Ariel Sharon "indirectly responsible" for the massacre, forever making his name anathema to the Palestinians and crippling his political career for the next 15 years.

In 1999, Israel began a unilateral withdrawal from the security zone in southern Lebanon, and the United Nations certified it had completed a full withdrawal from Lebanon in 2000. Hezbollah, a militant group that had formed during the Lebanon Civil War and had fought against the IDF, filled in the vacuum in southern Lebanon. Although the U.N. agreed that Israel had fully withdrawn, Syria and Lebanon continued to insist that a small piece of land on the border of Lebanon and the Golan Heights, known as the **Shebaa Farms**, was Lebanese territory still occupied by Israel. Israel continues to assert that it was in fact part of the Golan Heights and never Lebanese territory, and that Syria has manufactured the issue to give Hezbollah a pretext to continue attacking Israeli targets across the Lebanese border.

U.S. Secretary of Defense Caspar Weinberger meeting with Ariel Sharon in 1982

Chapter 12: Hamas

In 1988, a recently organized militant group issued its charter, which called upon Muslims to "raise the banner of Allah over every inch of Palestine." The group, an offshoot of the Muslim Brotherhood, declared, "Allah is its goal, the Prophet is the model, the Qur'an its constitution, *jihad* its path, and death for the sake of Allah its most sublime belief." Vowing to fight off the "Zionist invaders," the charter states, "The time will not come until Muslims will fight the Jews [and kill them]; until the Jews hide behind rocks and trees, which will cry: Oh Muslim! There is a Jew hiding behind me, come on and kill him!"

Despite having a charter that called for the murder of Jews across the world, Israel actually bolstered this fundamentalist religious group, universally known as Hamas, during its formative years in the 1980s. After occupying the Gaza Strip, Israel encouraged the rise of Islamists as a way of undercutting the secular PLO, which Israel had always viewed as the greater threat. One of the individuals who Israel helped was **Sheikh Ahmed Yassin**, leader of the Muslim Brotherhood in the Gaza Strip, who had organized a charity that built mosques, clubs, and schools there.

During the '80s, Sheikh Yassin built up military weapons caches, telling Israeli officials they were for use against the PLO, but when the First Intifada erupted in 1987, Yassin's charitable organization transformed into Hamas, a militant group that began carrying out attacks on Israeli targets. Israel arrested Yassin and began deporting Hamas militants out of the Gaza Strip. Meanwhile, Hamas began building a relationship with Hezbollah, situated across the Lebanese border to Israel's north.

Hamas has often taken pains to claim there is a distinction between its military branch, the Izz ad-Din al-Qassam Brigades, and its "political branch," but today the European Union, Canada, the United States and Israel have all designated the entire entity a terrorist organization. Since 1993, Hamas has launched dozens of suicide bombings and fired thousands of rockets at Israel, eventually replacing the PLO as Israel's biggest security threat among the Palestinian groups.

At the same time, relations between the PLO and Hamas remained chilly. Although the extent of cooperation between Hamas and Fatah during the '90s and early 2000s was disputed, the two sides eventually engaged in a civil war in 2007, with Hamas crushing Fatah's forces in the Gaza Strip and becoming the sole power in that territory.

Sheikh Yassin was the founder and ideological leader of Hamas until he was assassinated by Israeli forces in March 2004 following several suicide bombings carried out by Hamas. Yassin was a quadriplegic from the age of 12, needing a wheelchair to get around. Moreover, Yassin was assassinated as he was leaving morning prayers. The attack from an Israeli gunship killed several bystanders, and pictures of Yassin's wheelchair and corpse inflamed the Palestinians. Israel's attack on Yassin also drew widespread criticism across the globe.

Yassin was succeeded as the leader of Hamas by Dr. Abdel Aziz Rantissi, who had miraculously escaped an Israeli assassination attempt on June 10, 2003. Riding in the Gaza Strip, Rantissi saw an Israeli gunship fire a missile at his car. He quickly got out of the vehicle as it was destroyed and began running down an alley. The Israeli gunship then fired a missile into the alley at him, but he again narrowly escaped.

Rantissi stayed underground following that assassination attempt, only appearing in public at the memorial service for Yassin. Throughout March 2004 he stayed in hiding, only surfacing on

April 17, 2004 to visit his family. That was all Israel needed, hitting his car with a missile from a gunship and assassinating him.

Rantissi's assassination was a testament to the sophistication of Israel's intelligence agencies, the **Shin Bet** and **Mossad**, which have managed to infiltrate Hamas consistently. Hamas is acutely aware of it too: the group often executes individuals who it suspects are collaborators with Israel.

Chapter 13: The First Intifada

The **First Intifada** was a Palestinian uprising that broke out in 1987 against the Israeli occupation, triggering protests in the Gaza Strip, West Bank, and East Jerusalem. The Palestinians mostly protested with strikes, boycotts, and rock throwing, although Hamas and the PLO also engaged in violent attacks, including a suicide bombing, that killed over 150 Israelis. Underscoring the animosity between the PLO and the Islamic factions like Hamas and Islamic Jihad, intra-Palestinian violence also killed 1,000 Palestinians who were alleged to be Israeli collaborators. During the First Intifada, Israeli forces also killed over a thousand Palestinians.

By the time the First Intifada broke out, Jordan and Egypt had relinquished their claims to the West Bank and Gaza Strip respectively, leaving only the Palestinians asserting sovereignty over them against Israeli occupation. Although the PLO's leadership had been long ago exiled from the territories under Israeli control, the PLO became the de facto leader of Palestinian society in the territories, which improved their global standing.

The First Intifada was never a directly controlled uprising, and no Palestinian leaders expected it to make permanent changes in the ongoing conflict, but it was directly responsible for the Madrid Conference of 1991, which would put in motion all of the pieces that make up today's peace process formulations.

The most frequently invoked images of the First Intifada were ones like this, with burning tires and Palestinian youths hurling rocks at IDF forces.

Chapter 14: The Madrid Conference of 1991

The Madrid Conference is widely considered to be the first modern attempt to start a peace process through negotiations between the Israelis and representatives of the Palestinians. In October 1991, the United States and Soviet Union went about trying to bring Israel, the Palestinians, and other Arab nations like Syria, Lebanon, and Jordan all together in Madrid, Spain.

President George H.W. Bush was looking for an opening to finally settle the conflict after the Gulf War in 1991, using the "land for peace" formula that had been the centerpiece of Resolution 242. Though the conference eventually convened in November 1991, there was an issue over who could represent the Palestinians, since Israel distrusted the PLO. With the PLO's leadership still exiled in Tunisia, the Palestinian group included Palestinians who were not part of the PLO along with Jordanians, most prominently Saeb Erekat and Haidar Abdel-Shafi.

After the conference, the sides agreed to pursue negotiations on several levels, with the goal of establishing interim agreements that would later achieve a full peace that settled security issues, refugee issues, and economic issues. Although the aftermath of the Madrid Conference led to a peace treaty between Israel and Jordan in 1994, the other negotiations broke down.

One of the main stumbling blocks was Israel's 1992 elections. The incumbent government of Israel Shamir was led by the **Likud Party**, Israel's strongest conservative party, but he was being challenged by Yitzhak Rabin, who represented the **Labour Party**, Israel's main leftist party. Rabin was openly campaigning against the Likud's ongoing settlement policies, which were one of the main issues to be addressed by the negotiations between the Israelis and Palestinians. With the Israeli elections and that issue up in the air, progress was impossible.

Ultimately, the Madrid Conference did not lead to peace between the Israelis and Palestinians, but its formulations are still mainstays today. The Bush Administration had envisioned a peace process that would be solved by having the two sides negotiate interim agreements that would give the Palestinians self-government before attempting to tackle thornier issues like final borders, the fate of East Jerusalem, which the Palestinians wanted as a capital and the Israelis wanted to keep undivided, and the Palestinian right of return. These tougher issues became known as **permanent status issues**, now more often referred to as **final status issues**. The Madrid Conference also ultimately made Fatah the face of the Palestinians and thus the dominant political party, leading subsequent peace process attempts to designate Fatah as the Palestinian negotiating partner for the Israelis.

Saeb Erekat may not have officially been part of the PLO in 1991, but his participation at the Madrid Conference in 1991 and its subsequent negotiations made him a natural choice for the spot of chief negotiator in the Palestinian Authority established by the Oslo Accords in the mid-'90s. In addition to being the chief Palestinian negotiator at every major peace initiative of the last 20 years, Erekat is often the public face of the Palestinian government, making media appearances and giving the Palestinian viewpoint on issues to the outside world.

Chapter 15: Signing the Oslo Accords

Although the Madrid Conference was ostensibly a failure, secret negotiations between the PLO and the Labour leaders that formed the incoming Rabin government in 1992 were being conducted secretly in Oslo, Norway during 1992. Secret negotiations gave the sides the ability to avoid incurring political damage or public controversy over the terms being discussed, a tactic that had helped achieve the peace treaty between Egypt and Israel in 1978.

The Palestinian delegation, which included **Mahmoud Abbas**, and the Israeli delegation, which included Israeli Foreign Minister **Shimon Peres**, eventually reached an agreement on what became known as the **Oslo Accords** in 1993. The agreement even surprised the Clinton Administration, whose Secretary of State, Warren Christopher, had been part of the negotiations.

The Oslo Accords were a framework modeled after the goals of the Madrid Conference. The Accords provided for the establishment of the **Palestinian Authority (PA)**, which was headed by Yasser Arafat and Fatah. The Palestinian Authority would be given the responsibility for governing the Palestinians in the Gaza Strip and West Bank as the IDF gradually withdrew from parts of the territories and handed off security control to the PA. At the outset, the Israelis recognized the PLO as the Palestinian representative, clearing the way for the PLO's leadership to head the Palestinian Authority. Meanwhile, the PLO recognized Resolution 242, renounced terrorism, and recognized the right of Israel to exist in peace and security.

The Oslo Accords called for the IDF's withdrawal from parts of the territories in accordance with Resolution 242 over the course of a 5 year interim period, during which time the two sides were supposed to negotiate final status issues including East Jerusalem, Palestinian refugees, Jewish settlements, security, and final borders. These were deliberately left to be decided farther down the line, in order to give the parties room to generate progress and momentum during the initial steps that would make it more politically feasible for both sides to make tough choices.

On September 13, 1993, one of the iconic moments of the Middle East conflict took place in the Rose Garden, where Yasser Arafat shook hands with Yitzhak Rabin as President Clinton looked on. The signing of the Oslo Accords earned both men a Nobel Prize that year, like Begin and Sadat in 1978.

Then and Now:

Today, the issues of Jewish settlement growth and Israeli control over the borders of the Gaza Strip and West Bank have come to the forefront of the peace process, but in the Oslo Accords of 1993, the two parties agreed that settlements were a final status issue to be negotiated and that Israel would continue to be responsible for the borders of the Palestinian territories until a permanent agreement was reached.

The Palestinians continued to negotiate and sign agreements while Jewish settlement activity continued, until President Obama called for a freeze of all settlement activity in the West Bank and East Jerusalem in 2009. The Israelis viewed this as a radical departure from the peace process, and it also caught the Palestinians by surprise. As a result, the Palestinians began demanding a freeze of all settlement activity as a precondition before negotiations. Later in 2009, Palestinian Authority leader Mahmoud Abbas explained in an interview with a Washington Post reporter that Obama's policy had all but required him to start demanding a full settlement freeze as a precondition.

Chapter 16: Oslo Breaks Down

From the beginning, the Oslo Accords began suffering serious breakdowns. Israel's Likud party and other conservatives opposed the negotiations, which had barely passed Israel's Knesset. They also pointed to statements made by Arafat to Palestinian audiences in which he compared Oslo to a strategic truce signed by Muhammad with the tribe of Quraish that allowed Muhammad time to build up strength to vanquish his adversaries. Skeptical Israelis thus believed the Palestinians' goal was still to destroy Israel, and that the Palestinians simply viewed this as part of a gradual process that would make the end goal easier to accomplish. Meanwhile, Palestinians were skeptical that the Israelis would honor their side of the agreements, seeing resistance from conservatives and religious settlers in Israel as capable of derailing the Oslo Accords.

Moreover, the violence intensified after the Oslo Accords were signed. Most observers assumed that the violence was being carried out by extremists who hoped to stop the peace process, including Hamas and extreme Jewish settlers, but again both sides were skeptical that the other side was taking proper steps to guarantee security. The Palestinian Authority had renounced terrorism, but many in Israel now believed it was endorsing attacks, implying that Arafat and his group were complicit. At the same time, the "Cave of the Patriarchs" massacre in Hebron was carried out in February 1994 by extremist Jewish settler Baruch Goldstein, a follower of racist rabbi Meir Kahane and the Kach party, which had been banned in Israel in 1988.

Nevertheless, the two sides negotiated what came to be known as Oslo II, which were signed in Taba, Egypt on September 24, 1995. Oslo II established a detailed timeline that called for IDF forces to redeploy from certain areas of the Gaza Strip and Jericho in the West Bank, and eventually from major population centers in the West Bank, including Nablus, Kalkilya, Tulkarem, Ramallah, Bethlehem, Jenin and Hebron. Another phase called for the withdrawal of the IDF from about 450 smaller Palestinian settlements and villages in the West Bank.

Oslo II also established the idea of "safe passage," which would grant the Palestinians the ability to travel between the West Bank and Gaza, which were not connected by land.

On October 5, 1995, Prime Minister Rabin explained his rationale behind agreeing to Oslo II in a speech before the Knesset, outlining his vision of a permanent settlement with the Palestinians. Under Rabin's vision, Israelis would keep a military presence in the Jordan River Valley without annexing it, Israel would retain large settlement blocs near the Green Line, Jerusalem would remain undivided, and a Palestinian state would be demilitarized.

A month later, on November 4, 1995, Rabin was assassinated by a Jewish fanatic who sought to derail the Oslo Accords. Rabin's death was a huge blow to the Oslo Accords, even though his successor, Shimon Peres, attempted to continue moving the process forward. In May 1996, Peres lost the elections, as Likud leader Benjamin Netanyahu became Israel's new prime minister. An ardent opponent of the Oslo Accords, Netanyahu did agree to certain withdrawals after signing the Hebron Protocol and the Wye River Memorandum, but friction among his governing coalition made it impossible to continue withdrawals.

Important Notes:

Although the Oslo Accords did not end up creating a lasting peace, it is still technically in effect. Thus, when current Palestinian leader Mahmoud Abbas vowed to push for a unilateral proclamation of statehood via the United Nations, the Israelis complained that such a move would violate the Oslo Accords, which called for a negotiated peace settlement.

It is also interesting to compare Rabin's vision of a final settlement with the offer made by Prime Minister Ehud Olmert in 2008.

Rabin, a leftist Labour leader whose legacy is still viewed fondly across the globe as that of a peacemaker, called for an undivided Jerusalem, the retention of large settlement blocs, and a continued Israeli presence in the Jordan River Valley.

Olmert, once a Likud official who later joined Ariel Sharon's centrist Kadima Party, offered to divide Jerusalem with holy sites administered by an international committee, international forces stationed on the border with Jordan instead of Israeli forces, and the ceding of over 94% of the West Bank to the Palestinians, keeping about 6% for large settlement blocs while giving Palestinians sovereignty over an equal amount of land currently within Israel proper.

Although Rabin was a leftist and Olmert was a conservative, Olmert's offer was far more generous than the final settlement envisioned by Rabin. The difference indicates the extent to which the parameters envisioned in a final agreement have changed, a shift so great that the Labour Party of 1993 was further to the right on settling the conflict than the Likud Party was in the middle of last decade.

In a speech to Congress in May 2011, current Likud Prime Minister Benjamin Netanyahu laid out a vision almost entirely in line with Rabin's. Though the speech was warmly received by Congressmen in Washington D.C., political observers noted that it was completely unrealistic to expect it could ever form a basis for peace today.

Rabbi Meir Kahane formed the Jewish Defense League (JDL) in the United States, as well as the Kach party in Israel, eventually becoming a member of the Knesset in 1984. However, the radical rabbi was so far on the fringe that Israel banned his party in 1988. One of the members of Kahane's JDL was Baruch Goldstein.

On November 5, 1990, Kahane gave a speech to an Orthodox Jewish audience at the Marriot East Side Hotel in Manhattan. Following the speech, he was assassinated by El Sayyid Nosair, who walked right up to him and shot him dead on the spot.

Nosair was charged with murder but acquitted. However, Nosair would later be convicted of murder in the United States due to his involvement in the 1993 World Trade Center bombing, which was carried out by Ramzi Yousef. Yousef and Nosair both had ties to the "Blind Sheikh," Omar Abdel-Rahman, and Yousef's uncle is Khalid Sheikh Mohammed,, who masterminded the 9/11 attacks. Yousef, Nosair, and Rahman are all imprisoned for life, and Khalid Sheikh Mohammed will obviously be in custody for the rest of his days too.

Chapter 17: Barak's Offer at Camp David

Netanyahu's first term as Prime Minister was inconclusive, and he was soundly defeated in the 1999 elections by Labour leader Ehud Barak, a war hero of the Yom Kippur War and a former commando. Barak's election was seen as an opportunity to revive the peace process that had been flagging over the past few years.

Although the interim agreements that were to come first didn't go entirely according to the Oslo Accords plan, President Clinton invited Arafat and Barak to Camp David in July 2000 in an attempt to work out a deal on the final status issues. In a prepared statement before the negotiations began, both sides agreed "that negotiations based on U.N. Security Council Resolutions 242 and 338 are the only way to achieve such an agreement," and that both sides "understand the importance of avoiding unilateral actions that prejudge the outcome of negotiations and that their differences will be resolved only by good faith negotiations."

The four final status issues to be addressed were final borders, the fate of Jerusalem and the holy sites at the Temple Mount (which includes both the Al-Aqsa Mosque and Western Wall), the Palestinian right of return, and Israeli security concerns.

Borders

On the issue of borders, the Palestinians sought sovereignty over the entire West Bank and the Gaza Strip, telling the Israelis they would consider a one-to-one land swap with Israel that would exchange land within Israel proper to the Palestinians for land in the West Bank that already had major Israeli settlement blocs. The Palestinians also asserted that Resolution 242 called for full Israeli withdrawal from territories captured in 1967, which Israel claimed was an erroneous interpretation.

Barak offered Arafat a Palestinian state immediately on 73% of the West Bank and 100% of the Gaza Strip. Within the course of a few decades, the Israelis would gradually dismantle over 50 settlements and withdraw the IDF from more of the West Bank until the Palestinian state covered 90% of the West Bank. Israel would keep the major settlement blocs close to the border of the Green Line and give the Palestinians 1% of the Negev Desert as a land swap.

Barak also offered to create an elevated highway over Israel proper that would connect the Gaza Strip to the West Bank, in order to make it a **contiguous** state, the term most commonly used to mean the Palestinian state would be one continuous mass of land. The Palestinians argued that the offer would create disconnected clusters, often referred to as **cantons** or the more heavily charged term **Bantustans**, a loaded word that referred to apartheid South Africa, in which blacks were settled in a series of disconnected clusters. The Israelis and Americans both argued that the offer would have created a contiguous state.

Jerusalem

Jerusalem was the biggest sticking point for both sides. At the time, Israel was in control of the entire city and had annexed East Jerusalem, making it their undivided capital. Israel allowed a Palestinian mufti to oversee the operation of the Temple Mount, thereby giving the Palestinians authority over the grounds. But anytime there were disturbances or riots, Israelis retained the ability to shut down the Temple Mount from Muslim worshippers.

The Palestinians wanted complete sovereignty over all of East Jerusalem and the dismantling of the Israeli neighborhoods in that half of the city. The Palestinians proposed that Jewish holy sites in East Jerusalem would be under Palestinian sovereignty but would remain under Israeli authority, which would have the effect of a 180 degree turnaround of the current situation. The Palestinians would also have sovereignty over the Dome of the Rock, a holy site for both Muslims and Jews.

Barak tried to offer a situation in which the Palestinians would exercise self-government over the Palestinian population centers in Jerusalem, which would not technically divide the city but would have a similar effect. The Palestinians would continue to have custodianship without sovereignty over the Temple Mount, and the Palestinians would govern the Muslim and Christian Quarters of the Old City, while the Jewish and Armenian Quarters in the Old City stayed with Israel. The Israelis wanted to keep some major Jewish settlements near East Jerusalem like Gush Etzion, which were considered part of the West Bank but not Jerusalem, and in exchange Barak offered the Palestinians sovereignty over other villages that had been annexed into Jerusalem after the Six Day War but would now be given up by Israel.

The sovereignty and authority over Jerusalem's holy sites have also been sensitive issues for the Israelis because Jews were banned from worshipping at some of their most holy sites by the Jordanians from 1948-1967. Furthermore, Jordanian authorities defaced and vandalized some of the Jews' holy sites before being pushed out of Jerusalem in 1967.

The Palestinian Right of Return

Another major problem in the conflict is the issue of the Palestinian right of return. If all descendants of the Palestinian refugees were able to return to Israel, it would cease to be a Jewish state, which is clearly unacceptable to the Israelis. The Israelis also frequently point out that the 800,000 Jewish refugees from the 1940s have not been given a right of return to their old homes or been financially compensated for their forced expulsion. Meanwhile, the right of return represents a politically sensitive issue for Palestinian Authority leaders who don't want to be the ones to tell millions of their people that they cannot return. Israeli leaders often charge that the Palestinians won't give up the right of return because they realize it's their best chance to destroy the Jewish State of Israel, which many believe is still the ultimate goal of most Palestinians.

Barak envisioned negotiating a limited right of return that would look into allowing some Palestinian refugees back while compensating others, without allowing the Palestinian refugees to form a Palestinian majority in the State of Israel. The Israelis envisioned a situation in which about 100,000-150,000 Palestinians would be allowed to return to Israel, while contributing to an international fund that would financially compensate the other Palestinian refugees who made claims related to the right of return. Arafat discussed trying to set up a way in which the two sides would encourage Palestinian refugees to relocate outside of Israel, but he refused to sign an agreement that would not allow Palestinian refugees who wished to return to Israel to actually do so.

Israeli Security

Barak's offer called for a demilitarized Palestinian state, with Israel retaining a security presence along the Jordan River Valley. This would not allow foreign forces into the territories, and the only Palestinian forces would be security forces that would act like police forces in their own territories. The Palestinians and Israelis would both jointly operate border crossings, with the Palestinians running them while Israel observed them. Israel would have also reserved the right to deploy into Palestinian territories in emergency situations.

Settlement of All Claims

Since Israel was making an offer on the final status issues, one of the demands was that the Palestinians agree that it was a settlement of all claims, which would declare the Middle East conflict over. The idea behind this demand, which the Israelis included in subsequent peace offers, is that the Palestinian agreement to a settlement of all claims would prevent them from making further demands down the line. In other words, the Israelis were still skeptical that the Palestinians were only seeking a **two state solution**, not a temporary step toward destroying Israel itself.

Pointing Fingers

No peace deal was ever reached at Camp David in 2000, which led to finger pointing on all sides. Barak, Clinton, and some American negotiators like Dennis Ross claimed Arafat, who rejected the offer without making a counteroffer, was too intransigent. That viewpoint was echoed by Nabil Amr, a Palestinian Authority Minister in 2000. Others blamed the Israelis and Americans, including the Palestinians and prominent political observers like Norman Finkelstein. Barak's Foreign Minister, Shlomo Ben-Ami, would later say that if he was a Palestinian he would have rejected the offer too.

Although Camp David did not end with an agreement, Barak's offer set a minimum baseline for what subsequent Israeli prime ministers had to offer, which has gone a long way to shaping the international consensus on what a final peace deal should ultimately look like.

President Clinton at Camp David in 2000 with Barak and Arafat. Clinton would later write, "I regret that in 2000 Arafat missed the opportunity to bring that nation into being and pray for the day when the dreams of the Palestinian people for a state and a better life will be realized in a just and lasting peace."

Chapter 18: The Taba Summit

Despite the breakdown at Camp David in the summer of 2000, the Palestinians and Israelis negotiated at Taba in the Sinai Peninsula in January 2001, which is often considered the closest the sides ever got to reaching a deal. Throughout the rest of 2000, Clinton had tried to bridge gaps and put forth suggestions for the two sides to use at Taba, although he was leaving office and being replaced by George W. Bush.

Both sides agreed that the Green Line would be the starting point of negotiations, as well as the principle of "one for one" exchanges of land, now usually referred to as **mutually agreed land swaps**, but the sides disagreed over the extent to which Israel could exchange land for keeping certain settlement blocs.

Both sides also accepted Clinton's suggestion that the Palestinians and Israelis maintain sovereignty over Arab neighborhoods and Jewish neighborhoods in Jerusalem respectively, and the Israelis accepted that Jerusalem would be the capital of both states. This would have precluded an official division of the city.

On the issue of security, both sides negotiated cooperating jointly between their security forces in an effort to combat terror that was still being perpetrated by Palestinian militant groups Hamas and Islamic Jihad.

The other issues that had been raised and negotiated at Camp David were also discussed, including figuring out the right of return. However, before anything could be concluded, Israeli elections brought Likud leader Ariel Sharon to power, a response to the Second Intifada that had just started in late 2000.

Israel's negotiator, Foreign minister Shlomo Ben-Ami, would later state, "We made progress, substantial progress. We are closer than ever to the possibility of striking a final deal." Saeb Erekat, the Palestinians' chief negotiator, noting how close the sides were, asserted that the two sides would have needed only about 6 more weeks to draft an agreement.

Foreign Minister Shlomo Ben-Ami (left) shakes hands with Palestinian negotiator Ahmed Qurei (right) at the Taba Summit in 2001.

Chapter 19: The Second Intifada

Despite the intense negotiations that took place in 2000 and January 2001, the peace process was ultimately derailed during the Second Intifada.

Both sides have long argued over what triggered the Second Intifada. The Palestinian Authority claimed the Second Intifada was a natural, uncoordinated uprising triggered by Likud leader Ariel Sharon's visit to the Temple Mount in September 2000, as well as the inability to reach a satisfactory deal at Camp David the previous July. Palestinians in Jerusalem protesting Sharon's visit began rioting.

The Israelis would later assert that Arafat himself had planned the Second Intifada and that Palestinian leaders waited for the right moment to start the fighting. Fatah official Marwan Barghouti, later imprisoned by Israel for his role in attacks during the Second Intifada, later said, "After Sharon left, I remained for two hours in the presence of other people, we discussed the manner of response and how it was possible to react in all the cities and not just in Jerusalem." One of Hamas' top leaders, Mahmoud al-Zahar, also claimed that Arafat ordered Hamas and Fatah's militant wing, the al-Aqsa Martyrs Brigade, to begin launching attacks against Israel once he realized Camp David would not be successful.

Over the next three years, the fighting between Israelis and Palestinians reached a feverish pitch. The Palestinian Authority's Fatah launched attacks on civilians and IDF forces throughout the West Bank, including suicide bombings of civilian targets like pizzerias and buses. Hamas and Islamic Jihad also intensified suicide bombings.

In 2002, after a suicide bombing killed 30 Israelis during Passover, Sharon ordered the IDF to strike back with Operation Defensive Shield, a massive incursion back into the West Bank in places like Jenin and Hebron that had been turned over to the Palestinian Authority under Oslo. The climax of the campaign took place in house to house fighting in Jenin, where it was first believed that the Israelis had perpetrated a massacre that left thousands of Palestinians dead. It would later be determined that less than 60 Palestinians were killed in the fighting at Jenin, and over 20 IDF soldiers were killed there. Operation Defensive Shield ended with the Israelis killing hundreds of militants and arresting thousands of Palestinian fighters.

From a military standpoint, Operation Defensive Shield was a success, placing an iron grip over the Palestinian territories that made it much harder for the militant groups to launch attacks. But it did not quell the Second Intifada and only inflamed the Palestinians even more.

The Second Intifada began to gradually end around 2005, in response to several important changes. The intifada had discredited Arafat in the eyes of the West, and he was forced to appoint a prime minister for the Palestinian Authority, a spot filled by Mahmoud Abbas. Arafat himself would die in 2004, creating a void in Palestinian leadership that would look to be exploited by Hamas. The Second Intifada also demonstrated to Israelis that military force could be used to successfully prevent militant attacks but not help the peace process. And the Second Intifada was extremely deadly: the death toll is estimated to be upwards of 7,000 Palestinians and 1,100 Israelis.

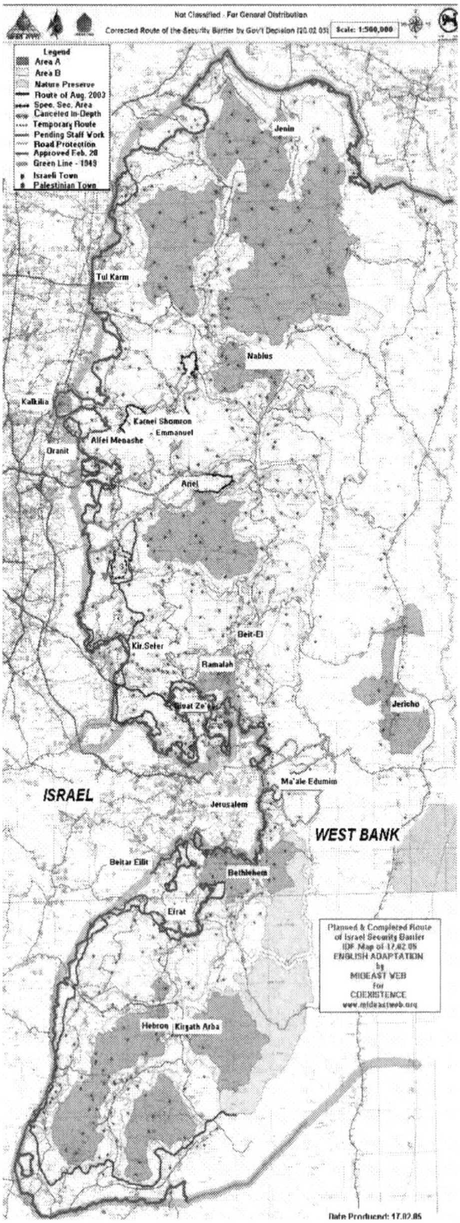
Not Classified - For General Distribution
Corrected Route of the Security Barrier by Gov't Decision (20.02.05)
Scale: 1:500,000
Legend
Area A
Area B
Nature Preserve
Route of Aug. 2003
Spec. Sec. Area
Canceled In-Depth
Temporary Route
Pending Staff Work
Road Protection
Approved Feb. 20
Green Line - 1949
Israeli Town
Palestinian Town
Jenin
Tul Karm
Nablus
Kalkilia
Karnei Shomron
Emmanuel
Alfei Menashe
Oranit
Ariel
Beit-El
Kir.Sefer
Ramalah
Jericho
Ma'ale Edumim
ISRAEL
Jerusalem
WEST BANK
Beitar Ellit
Bethlehem
Efrat
Planned & Completed Route
of Israel Security Barrier
IDF Map of 17.02.05
ENGLISH ADAPTATION
by
MIDEAST WEB
for
COEXISTENCE
www.mideastweb.org
Hebron
Kiryath Arba
Date Produced: 17.02.05

In response to the intifada, Israel built a barrier on its border with the Gaza Strip, which greatly reduced cross-border attacks into Israel from Gaza. Given that success, Israel began building a controversial barrier in the West Bank that ran along the Green Line but also cut into Palestinian land in the West Bank to protect Jewish settlements. The Israelis typically call it the **security fence**, while the international community and Palestinians often call it the **security barrier**.

The wall was condemned by the International Court in Hague, but the Israelis ignored the decision, having refused to participate in the case. When the complaint was brought to the ICC, Israel simply sent the wreckage of a bus that had been attacked by a suicide bomber to Hague and had it displayed outside the ICC for people to see.

In addition to activity at the ICC, the carnage wrought by the Second Intifada spurred the international community to political action, leading to the 2003 Road Map.

Chapter 20: The 2002 Arab Peace Initiative

In 2002, the Arab League met in Beirut and pushed forward a comprehensive peace initiative that would settle the conflict between Israel and the Palestinians, while normalizing relations between Israel and the rest of the Arab nations that don't yet recognize it.

The initiative's language for a peace agreement calls on Israel to do the following:

"(a) Complete withdrawal from the occupied Arab territories, including the Syrian Golan Heights, to the 4 June 1967 line and the territories still occupied in southern Lebanon;

(b) Attain a just solution to the problem of Palestinian refugees to be agreed upon in accordance with the U.N. General Assembly Resolution No 194.

(c) Accept the establishment of an independent and sovereign Palestinian state on the Palestinian territories occupied since 4 June 1967 in the West Bank and Gaza Strip with East Jerusalem as its capital.

In return the Arab states will do the following: (a) Consider the Arab-Israeli conflict over, sign a peace agreement with Israel, and achieve peace for all states in the region; (b) Establish normal relations with Israel within the framework of this comprehensive peace."

The Arab world continues to support the Arab Peace Initiative, reaffirming its support for the initiative in 2007, but Israel has never officially rejected or accepted it. While some of the framework may be included in a future peace deal, Barak's offer in 2000 demonstrated that Israel would not fully withdraw to the Green Line. Moreover, no major party in Israel accepts the Palestinian right of return in its entirety, because such a right of return would ensure that Israel would no longer be a Jewish state.

Chapter 21: The 2003 Road Map

In 2003, the international community, led by the **Quartet** of the United States, European Union, Russia, and the United Nations, tried to kick-start the peace process with what became known as the **Road Map for Peace**, which sought "a secure State of Israel and a viable, peaceful, democratic Palestine" that would help achieve peace and security across the Middle East.

The process became known as a road map in part because it called for phases in which the two sides would take steps together that would generate momentum and progress toward reaching the final status issues. The Quartet put it together by 2003 after the Israelis and Palestinians had been given the chance to discuss their concerns and obligations.

Phase I

In the first phase, the Palestinian Authority was to end the violence perpetrated not only by the al-Aqsa Martyrs Brigade but also groups like Hamas. The Palestinian Authority was also supposed to end incitement against Israel in its media and society, a reference to Palestinian shows glorifying jihad against the Jews. It also required the sidelining of Arafat by bringing Abbas to power.

Phase I also called on Israel to freeze settlement expansion and withdraw from Palestinian cities. Prime Minister Sharon confronted the Bush Administration over the language regarding the settlement freeze, with the two sides agreeing that the freeze would not preclude Israelis from building within preexisting settlements to accommodate the rising population. This became known as the **natural growth exception**, which allowed Israel to continue building within existing settlements. But Israel could not create new settlements or physically expand preexisting ones.

Phase II

Phase II envisioned an international conference that would help support a Palestinian economy while creating provisional borders for the Palestinian state. Other issues like sharing resources and security would also be negotiated between the Israelis and Palestinians during this phase.

Phase III

The final phase, which was intended to begin about a year after Phase I, was supposed to address the final status issues, including final borders, the fate of Jerusalem, the Palestinian right of return, the issue of Jewish settlements, and a region wide peace deal among Israel and its neighbors.

Israel's Reservations

Israel eventually accepted the Road Map in May 2003, but it attached 14 "reservations" along with its acceptance. These reservations included the requirement of all Palestinian militant groups being dismantled, the requirement that Palestine be demilitarized, the requirement that the Palestinians declare Israel's right to exist as a Jewish state, and that final status issues not be discussed prior to Phase III.

Of these, the one that has since become an issue is the requirement that the Palestinians declare Israel's right to exist as a Jewish state. To the Palestinians, it represented a brand new requirement that had not existed in Oslo or been brought up during Barak's peace offer at Camp David in 2000. To Israel, it is a way for the Palestinians to prove that their goal was a two state solution, not the destruction of Israel by demographically overwhelming it with the right of return of millions of Palestinians to create a Palestinian majority in Israel.

The Road Map Breaks Down

Sharon's government was skittish about the Road Map to begin with, and the Quartet quickly found it was hard to get either side to move on even Phase I. Whether the Palestinian Authority could stop attacks carried out by other militant groups like Hamas is still disputed, but as the Second Intifada continued to rage on during May 2003, the Israelis were reluctant to withdraw any further from the West Bank, arguing that it would only endanger Israel's security even more.

On February 13, 2004, with the Road Map ruined, the Bush Administration endorsed Sharon's new plan: a unilateral withdrawal of Jewish settlements from the Gaza Strip. According to the Bush Administration, "[N]egotiations were impossible because of Palestinian recalcitrance."

Mahmoud Abbas became the Palestinian Authority Prime Minister after the Quartet insisted on Arafat being politically removed from the scene. In 2003, it was unclear how much independence Abbas had within the Palestinian Authority, since Arafat had dominated Fatah for nearly 40 years. But when Arafat died in the Fall of 2004, it left Abbas as the de facto leader of the Palestinian Authority going forward.

Chapter 22: Israel's Withdrawal from the Gaza Strip

To Jews, the Gaza Strip had no religious importance or significance, which made Israeli leaders willing to withdraw from 100% of the Gaza Strip in negotiations with the Palestinians as far back as the Camp David Accords. In addition, the creation of the security barrier on the border had sharply reduced attacks across the border, which meant that attacks emanating from Gaza Strip would target Israeli settlers within the Strip itself. As a matter of security convenience, it was easier for the IDF to not have to defend settlements there and instead just man the border. Sharon also figured it would bolster Israel's standing in the eyes of the international community.

In 2004, Sharon's proposal for a unilateral pullout from Gaza was accepted by the government, but it was unpopular with his Likud Party, which induced him to break away from the conservative party to form the more centrist **Kadima Party**. Some Likud politicians like Ehud Olmert followed him, while others like Netanyahu stayed with the Likud.

Under the plan, settlers in the Gaza Strip were offered compensation to voluntarily vacate before August 2005. Those who didn't were forcibly removed by the IDF. By the end of September 2005, the removal of all settlers and settlements had been completed.

The plan also maintained the existing arrangements over the manner in which Israel imported goods to Gaza, provided water and electricity, and collected custom taxes. Israel controlled the Gaza Strip's border with Egypt, but Israel decided to cede control of it over to Egypt. At the time, Egypt's leader, Hosni Mubarak, feared the opposition group Muslim Brotherhood, which had ties to Hamas. In other words, the Israelis figured Egypt was motivated to prevent smuggling of weaponry into Gaza because Hamas was their problem just like it was Israel's. Israel continued to control the Gaza Strip's airspace and the coastal waters.

Given the manner in which Israel continued to control access to Gaza, the Palestinians and many human rights groups continue to insist that Israel still occupies the Gaza Strip, a characterization that Israel rejects.

Chapter 23: Bush's 2004 Letter to Sharon

Israel's unilateral withdrawal from the Gaza Strip pleased the Bush Administration, which was almost universally viewed as a very friendly (if not overly friendly) pro-Israel Administration. In fact, part of Sharon's motivation in pulling out of the Gaza Strip was that it came with certain understandings from Bush's Administration. After endorsing the withdrawal, on April 14, 2004, Bush wrote a letter to Sharon that marked important policy changes regarding how the United States viewed a final settlement.

On the issue of final borders, Bush's letter stated, "In light of **new realities on the ground**, including already existing major Israeli population centers, it is unrealistic that the outcome of final status negotiations will be a full and complete return to the armistice lines of 1949 [Green Line], and all previous efforts to negotiate a two-state solution have reached the same conclusion. It is realistic to expect that any final status agreement will only be achieved on the basis of **mutually agreed** changes that reflect these realities."

In essence, it became American policy that a final settlement would include Israel keeping its major settlement blocs in East Jerusalem and on the border of the Green Line. The phrase "new realities on the ground" still pops up often, a reference to the demographic changes in some Jewish settlements that have made them very large population centers.

The letter also provided a firm American position on the Palestinian right of return. The letter stated, "It seems clear that an agreed, just, fair and realistic framework for a solution to the Palestinian refugee issue as part of any final status agreement will need to be found through the establishment of a Palestinian state and the settling of Palestinian refugees there rather than Israel."

Chapter 24: Hamas Rises to Power

Part of the political reforms sought by the Quartet was that democratic elections be held in the Palestinian territories. The Quartet assumed that it would allow the Palestinian Authority to sort out its house politically while making them accountable to the Palestinians. However, 15 years of corruption had made the Palestinian Authority so unpopular among Palestinians that Hamas won a victory in parliamentary elections in January 2006, giving them a majority of seats in the government.

Taken aback by the results, Israel and the United States both refused to deal with Hamas, which was still sworn to Israel's destruction. As **preconditions** for negotiating with Hamas, the U.S. and Israel called upon Hamas to **renounce violence, recognize Israel's right to exist, and honor past agreements between Israelis and Palestinians.** Others held out hope that being in power politically would moderate Hamas' extremism. But immediately, Hamas leaders refused all of the preconditions.

Over the next half year, a major clash took place in the Gaza Strip after Hamas ambushed the IDF on the border by digging tunnels underneath it. A few Hamas fighters and IDF soldiers were killed, but Hamas also captured **Gilad Schalit**, an IDF soldier who was held in captivity until late 2011. Israel, now led by Ehud Olmert after Sharon suffered a stroke in January 2006, was unable to retrieve Schalit during a major offensive in the Gaza Strip.

Weeks later, Hezbollah launched hundreds of rockets at Israel and conducted a surprise cross-border raid that killed several IDF soldiers. The IDF was rushed into southern Lebanon, in the hopes of destroying Hezbollah. The war in Lebanon lasted nearly 2 months, but Israel was unable to destroy Hezbollah, which managed to fire thousands of rockets indiscriminately into Israel, forcing Israelis in the north to all but live in bunkers during the war.

The United Nations eventually brokered a ceasefire that called for stationing U.N. forces on the border to stand between Israel and Hezbollah, while also forbidding the shipment of weaponry from Iran and Syria into Lebanon. But not before Israel had done substantial damage to Lebanon's infrastructure, arguing that Lebanon was letting Hezbollah operate as a state within a state. Aiming to deter that situation and aiming to deter Hezbollah and Hamas from continuing rocket attacks and raids, Israel hoped that a heavy handed policy would work.

The fighting in Lebanon underscored important shifts in the Middle East conflict. First, it demonstrated Israel's inability to fully stop rocket fire into the country from the Gaza Strip or

Lebanon. Second, it indicated the extent to which Hezbollah, Hamas, Iran, and Syria were now all connected, posing grave security threats to the Jewish state.

Captured IDF Sergeant Gilad Schalit. The kidnapping of Schalit had been a hot topic in Israel since 2006, and Israelis considered the rescue or exchange of Schalit to be a national imperative. To prove he's alive and well, Hamas presented videos in which Schalit speaks and holds up a newspaper that displayed the date.

Shalit was finally freed in late 2011 in exchange for nearly 1,000 Palestinian prisoners, considered a victory for Hamas that would bolster its standing among the Palestinians.

Chapter 25: The 2007 Palestinian Civil War

After Hamas won the elections in 2006, tension between Fatah and Hamas continued to rise in the Gaza Strip. In addition to leaving the peace process stuck in mud, Fatah and Hamas began outright fighting throughout the Palestinian territories. Both sides began kidnapping and killing each others' loyalists and soldiers. Seeing Abbas and Fatah as the more palatable option, Israel and the United States continued to assist them against Hamas, giving them intelligence while also continuing joint security cooperation with Fatah's security forces that would help Fatah govern the Palestinian territories and keep Hamas' fighters at bay.

On February 2007, Fatah and Hamas reached a unity deal that created what was known as the Prisoners' Document, which called for the creation of a Palestinian state in the pre-1967 borders. Abbas signed it for Fatah and Khaled Meshaal, who had been exiled to Damascus years earlier, signed it for Hamas. The following month, a national unity government was formed, with Abbas still the Palestinian Authority Chairman and a Hamas dominated parliament.

The uneasy unity agreement held all of three months. In June 2007, war broke out in the Gaza Strip. 600 Palestinians were killed during the fighting, in which Hamas routed the Palestinian Authority and forced them completely out of the Gaza Strip. Abbas dissolved the government from the West Bank, but now Hamas was the sole ruling power in the Gaza Strip. The civil war in 2007 was particularly bloody, with both sides torturing their enemies, throwing them off buildings, and summarily executing them.

As a result of the civil war, the Quartet and Israel now found a situation in which the presumed Palestinian peace partner only controlled the West Bank, while Hamas remained defiant in the Gaza Strip and refused to acknowledge any of the demanded preconditions. The Bush Administration and Olmert's government began a policy of attempting to prop up the Palestinian Authority and the West Bank while isolating the Gaza Strip, hoping that the difference in quality of life between the two Palestinian territories would put pressure on Hamas in Gaza.

Khaled Meshaal, Hamas' political leader, was the target of one of the Israeli Mossad's most famous plots. On September 25, 1997, Mossad agents got into Jordan and held up a device to Meshaal's ear that transmitted a lethal nerve gas. Before they could get away, Meshaal's security guards were able to chase the Mossad agents and detain them with the help of Jordanian police. Meshaal had hours to live, and Jordan's King Hussein demanded that in exchange for the Mossad agents, Israel provide the antidote for Meshaal. Prime Minister Netanyahu eventually caved in, providing the antidote to Jordan that saved Meshaal's life.

In addition to providing the antidote, the agreement provided for the release from prison of Hamas' Sheikh Yassin.

Chapter 26: Olmert's 2008 Offer

Ehud Olmert was Prime Minister following Sharon's stroke, but political controversies hounded him throughout his time as prime minister, particularly old corruption charges. Olmert had also failed to meet his objectives in the 2006 intervention in the Gaza Strip and the fighting in Lebanon.

By 2008, Olmert was unpopular and it was clear that he would not be Prime Minister after the next elections. Foreign Minister **Tzipi Livni** indicated she would challenge Olmert for the top spot in the Kadima party, leading Olmert to announce on July 30, 2008, that he would not seek reelection.

Throughout that summer, an uneasy lull in violence mostly held between Israel and Hamas in the Gaza Strip. Meanwhile, Olmert began seriously negotiating a peace settlement with Abbas in the West Bank.

On the issue of borders, Olmert offered between 94-95% of the West Bank to Abbas, with Israel keeping major settlement blocs that held 75% of the Jewish population in the territories. Olmert's offer would have evacuated thousands of Jews in dozens of settlements along the Jordan River Valley. In exchange, Olmert offered a land swap in Israel equivalent to the West Bank territory Israel would keep, as well as a safe passage route from Hebron to the Gaza Strip through an elevated highway.

The offer was similar in other respects to Barak's offers in 2000. However, Abbas did not accept the proposed borders, later explaining that the Palestinians are seeking a mutually agreed land swap that would have Israel keeping about 2% of the West Bank for existing settlement blocs.

Once again, political ramifications and elections kept the two sides from continuing the negotiations, although they were getting closer to reaching an agreement. Olmert was unpopular at home, and elections were about to remove Olmert from power in favor of Kadima's Livni or Likud's Netanyahu.

Furthermore, Hamas had increased attacks from the Gaza Strip, shooting hundreds of rockets into Israel near the end of November 2008 and through December. Eventually, after a rocket killed an Israeli woman, Olmert ordered a massive invasion of the Gaza Strip, aiming to rescue Schalit, seriously cripple Hamas in the hope it might even help Fatah take Gaza back, and to establish deterrence to stop the incessant rocket firing. Over three weeks, *Operation Cast Lead* saw Israeli artillery pounding Hamas fighters, and Gaza's infrastructure.

Israel's offensive was controversial across the world, and the number of civilian casualties and charges of war crimes have been hotly disputed on all sides. However, from a practical political standpoint, Abbas could not be seen as being in cahoots with the Israelis while it was fighting other Palestinians. In that respect, the fighting in Gaza at the end of 2008 left the negotiations over Olmert's offer dead in its tracks.

The United Nations Human Rights Council (UNHRC) commissioned former South African Judge Richard Goldstone to investigate allegations of war crimes perpetrated by Israel in the Gaza war of 2008. During its history, the UNHRC gained a reputation as being a notoriously anti-Israel entity that had been chaired by human rights violators like Libya and Iran, Over 90% of its resolutions have singled out Israel for human rights violations. As a result, Israel refused to cooperate with Goldstone's investigation.

Goldstone's report, issued in September 2009, concluded that both Israel and Hamas had committed war crimes, although the report itself is almost entirely about the actions of the IDF.

Among the accusations it made against Israel, the report claimed Israel intentionally targeted Palestinian civilians. The fact finding in the Goldstone Report was disputed by Israel and much of it was debated by bloggers who could find inconsistencies in it through media reports of the fighting as it took place at the end of 2008.

The Goldstone Report's findings of Israeli violations were quickly endorsed by the UNHRC, who drafted a resolution that only went after Israel and did not mention Hamas. Goldstone criticized the UNHRC for selectively endorsing parts of his report. Meanwhile, Goldstone's personal reputation came under attack by Jewish groups, pro-Israel figures, and the Israeli government, who accused Goldstone of bias.

In April 2011, Goldstone authored an editorial in the Washington Post in which he acknowledged the report would have been different if he had known what he knew today. In particular, Goldstone walked back the charge that Israel intentionally targeted Palestinian civilians, claiming that was incorrect. Goldstone also praised Israel's internal investigations, contrasting them with Hamas' refusal to acknowledge the findings of the Goldstone Report as it related to them.

Goldstone wrote that he hoped there would be " a new era of evenhandedness at the U.N. Human Rights Council, whose history of bias against Israel cannot be doubted."

Chapter 27: Impasse in 2009

When President Obama took office, there was new hope that he would revive the flagging peace process, even though he was walking into an ugly situation that left the Palestinian territories divided between two warring factions, and the Israelis and Palestinians were still at odds over the formulation of all of the final status issues.

Obama spoke to the Middle East in June 2009 at Cairo that he hoped would help kick-start his foreign policy in the region. Shortly after Obama's speech, recently elected Israeli Prime Minister Benjamin Netanyahu gave a speech calling on the Arab world "to cooperate with the Palestinians and with us to advance an economic peace. An economic peace is not a substitute for a political peace, but an important element to achieving it."

Netanyahu's speech called for a two state solution, a first for a Likud leader. The speech also called for beginning negotiations without preconditions, but his speech outlined the history of the Middle East conflict that made it clear the Palestinians would have to recognize Israel as a Jewish state, and that the new state would have to be demilitarized so that it did not become another "Hamastan." In essence, Netanyahu had added preconditions, the latter typically being part of the security details that were to be negotiated halfway down the line as part of interim security arrangements or part of the issue of final borders that was a final status issue.

Complicating matters, Obama followed up his speech in Cairo by announcing a policy demanding that Israel freeze all settlement activities in the West Bank and East Jerusalem. Secretary of State Hillary Clinton also explicitly clarified that the settlement freeze also meant a freeze on the natural growth exception which had been reached between Sharon and the Bush Administration.

Obama's policy caught both sides off guard, since it was something the Palestinians had never demanded as a precondition to negotiations. For example, a freeze on settlement expansion was part of Phase I of the Road Map, which was to be done concurrently with the Palestinians making political reforms and ending violence. In Netanyahu's speech, he had stated, "We have no intention of building new settlements or of expropriating additional land for existing settlements." However, Netanyahu noted Israel's ongoing support for and reliance on the natural growth exception, adding, "But there is a need to enable the residents to live normal lives, to allow mothers and fathers to raise their children like families elsewhere." Thus, the policy created a substantial difference of opinion between Obama and Netanyahu, who also did not support dividing Jerusalem.

Netanyahu immediately rejected Obama's demand, but Obama's new policy also induced Abbas into making a full settlement freeze a precondition for negotiations with Israel. Abbas explained in 2009 and most recently in April 2011, "It was Obama who suggested a full settlement freeze. I said OK, I accept."

Chapter 28: The Settlement Moratorium in 2010

When Obama's Administration determined that it could not force Netanyahu to cave, in late 2009 it began seeking a 9 month moratorium on settlement activity to give the two sides a chance to begin negotiating. Netanyahu then proposed that Israel would freeze settlement activities for up to 9 months throughout the West Bank, except for housing units that had already begun being constructed in East Jerusalem. Secretary of State Clinton lauded Netanyahu's proposal as "unprecedented," but by then Abbas and the Palestinians viewed it as Obama caving in. Abbas explained, "We both went up the tree. After that, [Obama] came down with a ladder and he removed the ladder and said to me, jump. Three times he did it."

Throughout 2010, the United States had George Mitchell shuttle back and forth between the Palestinians and Israelis in order to keep at least some semblance of negotiations going. During the first 9 months of the year, Israel maintained its settlement moratorium, but it also announced plans to approve new units after the expiration of the moratorium.

In September 2010, the Obama Administration was able to get the two sides back to direct talks for the first time since Olmert's offer in 2008. The Administration hoped the direct talks would help push forward the framework for a final agreement within a year, but nobody remotely expected success. Moreover, Israel's moratorium was set to expire 3 weeks after direct talks started, and Abbas claimed the Palestinians would not continue direct negotiations unless it was extended.

The direct talks also had to deal with Hamas and Hezbollah, who vowed to derail them. Hamas carried out an attack in the West Bank for the first time in years, murdering Israeli civilians just as the talks were set to start.

The direct talks went nowhere fast. Netanyahu's demand that the Palestinians recognize Israel as a Jewish state was rejected by Abbas. Netanyahu's precondition actually goes toward resolving the Palestinian right of return, a final status issue, but at the same time Netanyahu had no interest in negotiating with a party that cannot at the outset say that Israel will remain Jewish after the peace agreement. On Jerusalem and final borders, the two sides were further apart than they had been in 8 years.

When the settlement moratorium expired, Abbas walked out on the negotiations. Obama attempted to get the Israelis to extend it another 90 days, but the Administration eventually gave up on that notion too, realizing that the two sides would find themselves in the same spot with the same problem regarding the moratorium 90 days down the road.

It's an open secret that Netanyahu and Obama do not see eye to eye and generally distrust and dislike each other. However, the strength of the alliance between Israel and the United States forces them to put on a happy face and work together.

Chapter 29: The Dueling Speeches of 2011

With negotiations at an impasse, Abbas began revving up a move for a unilateral declaration of statehood in 2011, a move that had been discussed with current Palestinian Prime Minister Salam Fayyad. For the previous 2 years, Fayyad had concentrated solely on building up political and economic institutions in the West Bank that would help prepare the Palestinians to hit the ground running on a new state. Although negotiations were dead, cooperation between the Israelis and Palestinians had mostly led to the economic peace that Netanyahu sought as a precursor to political peace, allowing Fayyad's projects room to grow.

To help their push, in May 2011 the Palestinians announced that they had reached a unity agreement between Fatah and Hamas, which had been sought by some members of the Quartet like the European Union as a helpful step toward allowing negotiations that would cover all of the Palestinian territories. However, others demanded that Hamas still renounce violence, recognize Israel's right to exist, and honor past agreements. Regardless, the unity government was reached to help bolster the Palestinians' push in the United Nations for a declaration of statehood, which is widely expected to easily pass the General Assembly and get vetoed in the Security Council by the United States.

That same month, Obama gave a speech that vowed to address popular uprisings across the Middle East, as well as the impasse between the Israelis and Palestinians. As it turned out, Obama's speech had important implications on U.S. policy toward the conflict. The statement that got the most attention was, "The borders of Israel and Palestine should be based on the 1967 lines with mutually agreed swaps, so that secure and recognized borders are established for both states." Netanyahu quickly attacked the statement, and a few days later, Obama clarified his statement before the pro-Israel lobby **American Israel Public Affairs Committee (AIPAC)**, seeming to walk it back by explaining that the issue of borders would continue to reflect the "new realities on the ground," thus suggesting that Israel would retain major settlement blocs.

At the same time, Obama's speech outlined a process in which a provisional Palestinian state would be created that would have the two sides agree on final borders before reaching an agreement on Jerusalem and the right of return. Israel saw this as a repudiation of Bush's 2004 letter to Sharon, but it would also have the effect of moving final borders from being a final status issue to the beginning of the peace process negotiations.

Obama also vowed to oppose the Palestinians' unilateral push for statehood, claiming only negotiations could reach a lasting peace. And Obama also questioned how Israel was supposed to negotiate with a unity government in which one of the partners did not recognize Israel's right to exist, although he did not explicitly spell out the three preconditions that the international community has historically required of Hamas.

Netanyahu happened to be on his way to the United States the day after Obama's speech, spending a weekend in Washington D.C. meeting with Obama before giving an address before a joint session of Congress. Obama's speech was criticized by prominent Democratic and Republican politicians, while Netanyahu received a bipartisan hero's welcome, and his speech received over two dozen standing ovations.

Netanyahu's speech echoed the preconditions his 2009 speech had, while vowing not to negotiate with Hamas, which he labeled "the Palestinian al-Qaeda."

The tension between Netanyahu and Obama in their White House meeting after Obama's speech was palpable. Before reporters, Netanyahu lectured Obama on how the 1967 borders were "indefensible" while a clearly displeased Obama looked on.

Chapter 30: Impasse at the U.N.

Despite all of the international lobbying conducted by the United States and Israel in an attempt to head off the Palestinians' unilateral bid for statehood at the United Nations, Abbas went ahead with his bid in September 2011. Much to the chagrin of Obama and Netanyahu, Abbas' attempt was widely supported across the world. The welcome that Abbas received at the General Assembly was every bit as warm as Netanyahu's was before Congress just four months earlier.

Why would the Palestinians go to the U.N. after Obama had made clear for months that the U.S. would ultimately veto any attempt at Palestinian statehood in the Security Council, which would singlehandedly prevent the Palestinians from being granted statehood?

Bringing Pressure to Bear

With most of the world supporting his bid, including a sizable majority of the General Assembly, Abbas was acutely aware that Obama hoped to avoid reaching the point at which the U.S. would have to use the veto in the Security Council, which would bring global criticism. At the same time, putting the Palestinian cause front and center naturally brought more pressure to bear on Israel and the Netanyahu administration. Abbas said as much himself, explaining that he hoped the statehood bid would allow the Palestinians to take claims against Israel to the ICC, as well as put them on equal footing with Israel in negotiations.

The Palestinians' unilateral push for statehood in the U.N. without negotiating with Israel was viewed by some as a risky gambit for Abbas, especially since it was clear beforehand that the Security Council veto would unquestionably happen. But it had the desired effect of putting political pressure on Israel and the Quartet to scramble to attempt to resolve the impasse. French President Sarkozy and Obama attempted to work out a framework in which the two sides would begin direct negotiations again, hoping to reach an agreement within a year. Naturally, this was viewed as wildly unrealistic, and although Netanyahu expressed willingness to reenter direct negotiations with the same caveats he had voiced in 2009, Abbas continued to refuse negotiations of any type until Israel halted settlement construction.

Going Nowhere

As of December 2011, all parties remain stuck at the current impasse. The Palestinians' statehood bid is still before the U.N., and Israel continues to complain that the unilateral attempt to get statehood at the U.N. represented an end-run around negotiations that violated the Oslo Agreements.

Nevertheless, the Palestinians have gained political advantages with their push. The **United Nations Educational, Scientific and Cultural Organization (UNESCO)** recognized the Palestinians as a state, earning loud condemnation from the United States, and Congress threatened to cut all funding to the UN organization.

Moreover, the longer the impasse remains, the more pressure has been brought to bear on Netanyahu's administration. Although Obama faces a tough reelection, and analysts believe he doesn't want to potentially alienate Jewish voters by taking a tough stance on Israel, senior administration officials continue to take Israel to task for what it sees as Netanyahu's unwillingness to reengage the Palestinians. In December, Secretary of Defense Leon Panetta called on Israel to "get back to the damn table" with the Palestinians, despite the fact it is Abbas that continues to refuse to negotiate without a settlement halt.

Chapter 31: The Outstanding Issues Left

At the end of May 2011, it seems the Middle East conflict is further away from being resolved than ever before. Here are some of the issues in the region still outstanding that need to be addressed.

The final peace agreement: It is often said that everyone knows what the final peace agreement will look like, and there is indeed a consensus that there will be a limited right of return, final borders that resemble the Green Line with mutually agreed land swaps, and some sort of sharing of Jerusalem. However, neither side currently believes the other wants those, and political concerns also restrict the extent to which the sides can make concessions on issues like Jerusalem and the refugees.

Israel and Syria: Any peace deal between Israel and Syria will require the return of the Golan Heights. However, this is complicated by the existence of Hezbollah, which is so intimately tied with Iran and Syria that it is practically a proxy army in southern Lebanon along Israel's border. The West has tried and so far failed to peel Syria away from its alliance with Iran, and Syria faces serious political upheaval with protesters and violence.

Hamas and Fatah: It remains to be seen whether the two Palestinian factions will actually work together or trust each other, or whether a unity government between the two that puts on a united front will suffer a "mask slipping" moment, as it did in 2007.

Demographics: Over a million Palestinian Arabs still live in Israel and even hold Knesset seats, while several million live in the West Bank. It is often argued that the rising Palestinian population in the West Bank will eventually mean there's a Palestinian majority in Israel and the West Bank. Obama made this claim in his May 2011 speech. The idea is that if the Palestinians in the West Bank outnumber the Jews in Israel and the West Bank settlements, Israel as an occupying force at that point will become an apartheid state and cease to be a democracy.

People continue to dispute whether the population rates and demographics will ever actually lead to a Palestinian majority in Israel and the West Bank, but it's a fear that caused radical philosophical changes in Likud leaders like Ariel Sharon. Many Israelis fear that the Palestinians continue to refuse offers in the hope of dropping demands for a two state solution and instead seek one bi-national state for both the Palestinians and Jews. With a Palestinian majority, Israel would cease to be a Jewish state.

BULGARIA
Skopje
Istanbul
Bursa
Ankara
Izmir
TURKEY
Konya
Adana
GEORGIA
Tbilisi
ARMENIA
Yerevan
Baku
Caspian Sea
Tabriz
UZBEKISTAN
TURKMENISTAN
Ashgabat
Tashkent
Bishkek
KYRGYZSTAN
Dushanbe
TAJIKISTAN
Kashi
Aleppo
Mosul
Kirkuk
SYRIA
Nicosia
CYPRUS
Beirut
Damascus
IRAQ
Baghdad
Tehran
Mashhad
Kabul
AFGHANISTAN
Islamabad
Esfahan
IRAN
Kandahar
Lahore
Quetta
Tel Aviv-Yafo
ISRAEL
Jerusalem
Amman
JORDAN
Alexandria
Cairo
Al Jizah
Al Basrah
KUWAIT
Kuwait
Shiraz
New Delhi
PAKISTAN
EGYPT
SAUDI ARABIA
BAHRAIN
Manama
Persian Gulf
Abu Dhabi
Riyadh
Doha
QATAR
UNITED ARAB EMIRATES
Muscat
Karachi
Jaipur
Ahmadabad
Aswan
Red Sea
Jiddah
Mecca
OMAN
Port Sudan
Mumbai (Bombay)
Pune
Omdurman
Khartoum
ERITREA
Asmara
YEMEN
Sanaa
Arabian Sea
SUDAN
Aden
Gulf of Aden
DJIBOUTI
Djibouti
Socotra (YEMEN)
Addis Ababa
Berbera
LAKSHADWEEP (INDIA)

Made in the USA
Columbia, SC
02 January 2020